Facing West

ALSO BY KELVIN CORCORAN

Robin Hood in the Dark Ages
The Red and Yellow Book
Qiryat Sepher
TCL
The Next Wave
Lyric Lyric
Melanie's Book
When Suzy Was *
Your Thinking Tracts or Nations
New and Selected Poems *
Roger Hilton's Sugar
Backward Turning Sea *
Hotel Shadow *
Words Through A Hole Where Once There Was A Chimpanzee's Face
For the Greek Spring *
Radio Archilochos
Sea Table *

Titles from Shearsman Books

Kelvin Corcoran

Facing West

Shearsman Books

First published in the United Kingdom in 2017 by
Shearsman Books
50 Westons Hill Drive
Emersons Green
BRISTOL
BS16 7DF

Shearsman Books Ltd Registered Office
30–31 St. James Place, Mangotsfield, Bristol BS16 9JB
(this address not for correspondence)

www.shearsman.com

ISBN 978-1-84861-523-6

ACKNOWLEDGEMENTS
With many thanks to their editors some of these poems have appeared in the
following magazines: *Molly Bloom, Black Box Manifold, Tears in the Fence, Free
Verse, The Fortnightly Review, Snow.*

An earlier version of *Radio Archilochos* was published by Maquette Press
in 2014, with my thanks to Andy Brown for his companionship
in this and other ventures.

The painting on the cover is *Halla Study*, 2005, by Brian Rice.
I am very grateful to him for his generous agreement to its use.

Contents

The Abduction Zone

The Abduction Zone

After Argos Io really was in Egypt
sand in her mouth, sperm in her lap;
she took the wet with the dry
a preservative in the Nilotic oven.

She wasn't caught in another account,
unlike Helen of the different narratives;
she was there, she ran or was abducted
Greeks asserted as self-serving ambiguity.

Though the names have changed since then
you can go there, see the long lick of the river,
the deep horizon, cold stars, the bull of Apis,
hear the creak and splash of waterwheels.

Io didn't feel like a figure in myth,
a clause in the east-west see-saw shuffle,
no boustrophedonic ur-text girl;
she liked her nails and mouth neat and red.

I'm a king's daughter, she said,
give me what I want, I don't trade;
the tender little quail for dinner
and at night that one-string song.

*

Then the ancient world wavered
in the voice of Roza Eskenazi,
her volatile rhapsody might breach
the barriers of expectation.

A song circles the harbour wall,
Greek night blackens the village,
the little owls call, dogs die, new breeds run
and Roza my child sings on the edge.

Then the ancient world, who sailed by here?
Oh Cleopatra, that we perish, talk to him;
take our kind tender for the distant dead
their white selves walking against the sky.

Their unaccountable emotional quality,
their feet sliding on the waves;
illegible their names, the distant dead
come calling in an unimaginable tongue.

*

Theseus abandoned Ariadne on Naxos
by the harbour, to the rocks and swine;
the dancing god in bloody riot arrived
and she screamed her head off.

I can't stay here, counting village idiots,
smelling pig flop and that effeminate stranger
spraying the asphodel like a tomcat;
the sea blinds me, the sail-away sea gone sour.

I trip on the beating tide, sway like a tree,
there's no centre here, just rock and wind and salt;
I see the drowned temples of white forgetting
where nameless creatures feed and fuck.

Ariadne really couldn't live there,
so it ended in the olive grove on the hill;
she stepped off the dithyramb into thin air
the sea winking blue all around.

*

Where Ritsos fought and stood aside
where imprisonment drilled his brain,
they've built a monkey house
a monument to fake money and nepotism.

*

Europa swam into Ovid's arms
the sea's crowded and I can't get o'er
the sea surges flooding all the time
a girl wide-eyed as if it all just began.

*

Doctors redeployed to avoid the sick
a swimming pool tax for others,
the scabrous rash of shoddy houses
begins the rot as future option.

*

Reports all along the Pylos coast
last offerings gold scrap metal victims
ships from where? raiders? burning?
light beacons, mobilise, burning, stop.

*

So what are we doing now Potnia?
Do you see them at the foot of the hill
surrounding us, a flood, do you see them
through our transparent walls?

Slaves to an alien code, eyes shining,
mythographers bound and hungry:
will they come to care for purple robes?
Either way, at present, it's of no comfort.

May as well dance on sea glint
and expect to stay dry, return home,
prosper beyond the long shadow
occupied by courtyard stir only.

Lady we kept true to you
in the high places where light is born
and in the caves of bloody earth
breathing, we kept true to you.

*

A warm wind crosses the Hellespont
but subtle rather, a breeze hesitating
slips into the long reaches of the afternoon
and the blue margin between two worlds.

And I remember my submission to you;
it was always there, its slow message rides me,
an inclination in my limbs, just let go love,
then hurtling down hill at the tilt of your head.

You're out there now, a black dot above the splash;
the better swimmer cutting a V, will I ever catch you?
It's a large body of water and deep enough,
on the other side, in the dark village, we'll rest.

That's the trouble, she said, I breathe this element
but where do you start with a founding myth?
These waves absorb me, drown my secret names,
and the last thing I saw – a golden beast swimming.

*

With our expansion westward we found the Sikels,
not even peasants, primitives living in ditches;
what they'd do for some pottery and metalwork.

We mapped out the edges, the coastline and inlets,
never what we really did in there for diversion;
the silver sea to the ends of the earth tricked us.

There's an art to founding a city and an art to forgetting,
our music was in despair, ruined and irrelevant,
even the thought of song scattered to the rim of our lives.

*

So one day there you are out in the meadow
friends together collecting the pretty narcissi,
counting rows of cabbages down to the river;
you laugh and cast lots for sex, for business.

You wave at the coloured yachts gliding-by,
Life's Promise, Bright Dawn, perfect names for fun;
and the little rowing boats like breathing
ascend mesmeric into the broad paths of heaven.

Then cataclysm – smashed face down in the dirt,
eye to eye with the roots of irrelevant plants,
their little white teeth snapping underground;
you see the hole in the dark heart of everything.

Of course this is Persephone's practiced song;
as the lights burn low in our buried gardens
and memory flits from gate to gate in rounds,
we're all singing – no we'll not come back again.

*

Hermes donned his cloak, primed his sandals
and lifted the baby onto his shoulders;
for the rest they were naked, at ease.

The baby reached for the cluster of grapes,
ready to drink a river and take possession;
but where were they going at such speed?

Though there was talk of escape and rescue,
looking at them you sensed the baby held sway,
a radiant beam trailing across the blue.

.   .   .

Hermes was rescuing the twice-born Dionysus from divine slaughter.
Some of the dazzling wonder of Praxiteles' statue is the baby's innocence
of this circumstance and of his own growing power. Compiling the
various versions of their journey would make the sky look like an air
traffic control screen at the height of summer. The flight is the point,
and a youth rescuing a baby, a god always arriving – a double promise
of life.

*

So another day, and there you are in the meadow,
not particularly aware of the archetypal frame,
again a flower picking scene, this time by the sea;
normality at rest in the shadow of father's house.

The white event tiptoed in suggesting dressage,
his mighty breath barely stirring the daisies;
oh feel his soft nose, his chains of dribble stiffening,
an electric shiver ignites his muscled flanks.

Hold on girl, he groaned, plunging up and down,
we might hit turbid water the way we're going;
see that island there floating free in the blue,
between Asia and your name we're surely bound.

Once on land Europa never looked back at all;
subsequent events proved she had a strong stomach
– and a good deal of curiosity: she became a queen,
eyes wide she surveyed the court and liked it.

*

Antiope

Four syllables you slug,
say it Ἀντιόπη An ti o pe
a voice at night opposed
could storm a city

Antiope, her trickster
and their versions, a voice at night
a shower of arrows
razor confetti falling

As always, this question
from the abduction zone
did she go to him?
did he steal her away?

*

a horse that runs in dreams

a find
          fields and fields
of votive horses
                    sprightly black

*

She swore by the dark bed of Persephone
she'd had enough of village boys,
their dumb plucking on banjos.

Give me one who can move at speed
who looks like he can wear a haircut,
give me a horse that runs in dreams.

*

She would listen to country music driving home,
decisions made, hands steady, tuning in and out;
certain colours worked for her on the windscreen,
the headlights reaching forward into the future.

White – meaning blue of the familiar hills,
darkness rushes by like a bow wave forgotten;
from a capsule of dials and calibrated thought
she splashes home to open her mouth and speak.

I heard this song on the radio, I just
I thought it was but no, I don't know,
it filled my head, I just wanted to be here,
the road a lyric, like the wings of song.

Dionysus

Dionysus begins the action by walking on stage;
standing there, frank, androgynous, slender as a snake:
I am Dionysus – and they threw the stranger in prison.

I am Dionysus – and Thebes took off enraptured,
a seismic ripple rolled around like a boiling sea
stirring the poor out of town dressed in goatskin.

Everything went lopsided, the city walls, the women,
a thought tearing the air and the pines bending low,
foxes, dogs, horses blew trumpets and ran in mad circles.

Then Dionysus pursued the action in absolute terms,
light fingered the vine, agon, stop, kill a fool or two, over;
and the leaves clapped their varnished little hands.

At last the earth's many mouths gaped blood hungry,
dark song of smoke rose, pretty wing pretty wing;
her wreathed face held in the mind half a life.

*

We'll come to Cadmus arriving and departing,
as hard as ABC and the hierarchies of meaning
smack you in the face in yet another storm,
to find an account of the alphabet in waves;
ropes sing, big sail billows beating across the world,
and always, the sound the waves make shaping thought.

The wind hit them broadside, skidding on the water,
askew the elliptical grain, down into the glossy trough;
pulling the steering oar for endless correction
they sailed westward – and like a feature in experience,
his back fairing hand traced rounded circles and scratches,
at first light engraved a lexicon, trade routes and ascent.

Cadmus – what have you caught in your net?
Big trouble language and its aetiology,
buried sinews, a god and indifferent fish?
You'll sleep on bare salt-encrusted rock,
limbs stiff entangled, dream of artful speech
and the river running about the earth articulate.

*

Nonnos claims Harmonia was spoken to by her foster-mother in a clever imitation of speech, an eastern mode of beckoning. She explained everything but the girl would not have the stranger. She was not mad about alphabet boy.

But there he stood, gold in his body, persuasion in his mouth. Desire licked at Harmonia and then bit and it changed her heart. She kissed her country's dust goodbye and one morning in the season of fair sailing, she went down to the sea with him. At this point, with her first step onto the unstable deck of the little ketch, she understood the nature of myth and volition. She was herself and not herself, the material of the deep song always sounding. Harmonia and her boy would have happily drowned themselves together.

The boat was a common trading vessel. It was full of strangers and crammed with the gifts of Sidon; a graven model of speaking silence, a notion of connected harmony and other goods – copper, wax and dye. These things, and a band of men, were needed to found a city and forget seafaring. Cadmus kept her untouched and they sailed for Hellas.

In their long life together she always thought of him walking out of the saffron valleys of Cilicia. This was before their time in Illyria as snakes in the underworld. And Harmonia would say – Hey Cadmus, do you hear our rhythm dah de dah de, our cart bouncing out of Thebes and the mounting waves of memory and forgetting, dah de dah de?

*

The war is perpetual but interrupted occasionally by peace or mere exhaustion and stand-off. I think it may have always been this way. Ten years of war and ten years to reach home, as preface to continuation. In *The Women of Troy* Euripides depicts the required murder of Andromache's infant son. Her husband is dead, Troy is gone in rubble and smoke, the women and children are enslaved – "The Achaeans are carrying home their property." The child is to be thrown from the battlements, lest he rise a future king against the Greeks. We understand this as a pre-emptive strike. Andromache says to her son, put your arms around my neck one last time and let me smell your sweet skin. This is a different order of reality beyond the ops room, the peace conference, the cockpit.

The young are slung by their clean little heels into the grinder. The slinging is largely a matter of ideology and the protagonists in charge agree how to set about this. There they go, the keen unblemished youth, whoosh like stars into the furnace. The pleasure in eviscerating the enemy isn't denied but is best enjoyed by proxy, by proclamation and broadcast. You survive by staying out of the lists and remote from prefabricated thought. Though the bloody dance is everywhere, spraying body parts centrifugally, writing the red words all over the shop from here to Timbuktu. Come little one, let me smell your sweet skin one last time.

*

I can find no account of Persephone's return from the underworld
it must have been on that first day the ground did not open for descent.

She walked in the Spring meadows of Hellas with no shadow in mind
alive in the total field to feel every blade of grass turn and flow and soften.

The ripe cud of it invaded her hands and flooded her nerves in one wave,
light running like a river in every element of the field of the whole world.

*

Battened down in the house all week, buried
at night the wind roaring us into the waves,
thunder rattled the roof, rain blinded the windows
and in sonic troughs mountains collapsed.

The storm spoke darkness in our dreams,
blew thought to pieces, the season torn apart;
daybreak drained colour from the sky in holes
and the olive trees dance blasted a crop.

Slowly music infiltrated the air
returned the first experience of sound
the rules of the anthropometric world,
all distance washed away around the cape.

ο καιρός the meteorology of gods
dictates a climate of unusable terms,
all along the coast to Trachila,
the sea reclaims its default blue for blue.

*

I was in a light aircraft with my dead parents,
I think it was them, I could tell it was my mother,
the way she held herself, her look and dark hair.

I had a small rucksack with a parachute packed inside,
it kept changing, a cocktail umbrella, a delicate parasol
then a parachute again; timing matters here, I thought.

My mother said – *But you're always going away.*
I said – *I know but I really don't want to.*
Then out into the darkness all the way down.

On the tilting ground of roads and revealed borders,
I was staring up into the dark sky of the absent ones;
they circle the earth to spot us and we never see them.

*

There are crossing points and they belong to Artemis;
any journey is an accumulation of crossing points.

They are marked by shrines, hidden tunnels and entrances,
the trash of sacrifice embedded in the mass of fibrous roots.

From Argolid to Arcadia, from Messinia to the end of the land
we drive the empty post-crash roads of ruined commerce.

Through the deep catalogue of our dealings and mineral certainty,
Artemis, torch bearer, depicts the lot of us moving off.

The journey is never personal – and is always personal,
a hole tapped in the skull, a child curled by her mother.

Our actions autonomous, joined, as if by thermal imagery,
the heat conveys red purple red our dance on hollow ground.

The road takes a final turn to Matapan and the double sea,
enters the inhabited darkness dressed in beads of light.

*

Two old men talk dressed in fawn skins,
holding wands, ivy crowns their heads;
– But the very thought of dancing, cut and caper
makes me falter, it's not for me.

– Come on, let's get on with it, just a few steps,
up the mountain and show respect.
We think them old and foolish, twittering,
then the bloody fool enters and takes charge.

Up there on Cithaeron rivers run, women run
without memory and smiling confinement,
pines waver, animals feed, that song sounding;
come on, step up, show respect.

*

We're here for anthropomorphism to deliver its low blow
and see abstraction cartwheel across Arcadia;
but to stand aside, conducting the disquisition
abandons the figure of the journey and its meaning.

And without asking - what do we know and for how long?
the moment of our jangling limbs is certain, the journey fixed;
my girls walking ahead into the dark streets, baby in arms,
his bright face scanning the whole world for clues.

*

Ino took on her dead sister's baby, she had no choice,
the one unharmed by the thunderbolt that orphaned him.

Keep him safe, urged Hermes, as he landed out of the blue,
– You'll inherit the sea, the story of your sisters, Ino of the waters.

She kept him indoors, unseen by sun or moon,
those drones of spiteful gods plotting smoky vectors.

Dionysus, bright light, you beacon face darling, she sang;
the boy never slept, full of leaping life and hard to hide.

Later, driven to streaking madness by Hera, Ino ran,
her own son, tortured Melicestes, wrapped in her arms.

Under a spinning sky she saved him from her husband,
and mocked by her sister, hurtled the air into whiteness.

She curled her toes over the bite of volcanic rock,
took her dive and entered the deep as Leucothia.

Meanwhile Dionysus lounged in the fields of Lydia,
blossomed and swam in the rolling golden river.

Cushioned by roses and lilies on the dewy banks,
he auditioned his party friends for orgy and riot.

– Hang around, blow a flute, flick a drum, he said.
– Oh she's nice, he said, and the celebrity circus moved on.

Before, Ino had a hand in the dismemberment of Pentheus,
grasped and tore and danced the scatter dance in the meadow.

Inos meaning sinew, erotic prompt, the many versions manifest
but none of this is reliable, just dubious etymology, speculation.

As Leucothia she ran atop the white waves and found her name;
her life was in the sea, diving to save the drowned.

Under a spinning sky she hurtled pliant into whiteness,
ready for the dive, Ino of the waters, Leucothia of the deep.

*

Indeed Dionysus seems always on tour, rolling into town,
India, Thrace, Thebes, Crete, various islands, like a rumour;
leaving a trail of dead women discarded, as if in a ballad,
Dionysus with his village song and clodhoppers ascendant.

Dionysus is always arriving somewhere, hennaed, pissed,
his mouth in our mouths – sings, *let the vines grow over me;*
surrender, whether you surrender or no, the oyster his world,
what's not in his hands, made-up, comforting gibberish.

Dionysus, standing there, says – *water won't slake it,*
his middle dynamic like background hum ineluctable;
Lydia, Phrygia, Persia, Bactria and Arabia claim him
launched from the Asian seaboard like a prick torpedo.

Orpheus/If I could

Morning of birds and sea sound
on three sides surrounds us,
the sun lays a path through milkwort and daphne;
barely on land at all, a ruined country at our backs
where some lives survive.

Morning of birds, pigeons of the tower,
bonny sparrows and various warblers
weave and chip the air of sea sounding;
to walk along the spit from the peninsula
face west, catch the literal song of spring.

*

Orpheus
          of the scattering
Orpheus
          of song
          of the power over beasts
Orpheus, wry-necked
          from the underworld.

Which is what we know
not the closed mouth mystery,
the torn sounds of song.

Separate scattered singing atoms
that blackbird this morning
and once I heard ... gone.

There was a child in a garden,
once I heard that long note
was it the air in a long note?

Like the boundless young sky,
Or phe us
of the bloody spouting tree.

*

Son or pupil of Apollo,
husband to Eurydice,
son of the muse of epic poetry:
name of obscure origin.

Orphne: darkness or night;
his journey to the underworld,
his initiations conducted by night,
origin of the English word – orphan.*

*(Thus, for instance, Frank O'Hara
discovered his genius.

'If anyone was looking
for me I hid behind a
tree and cried out, *I am
an orphan.*'

And it's always crowded
behind those trees,
all of us orphans dancing
– and the trees dancing.)

*

Mycenaean tholoi tombs
stationed across the hills
radiant bones, gold, weapons.

An entrance, a passage, a chamber
ritual of crossing points,
ritual of what is done.

We went down into the fields
to talk the quiet word
to feed them and lay gifts.

*

Orpheus walked the dark path
through black trees arching,
their bloody roots like shadows
seeping deep entangled underground
where the light collapsed in stripes.

The earth gives way at every step,
foot sinks, birds stop singing;
in that silence Orpheus said to himself
– My heart's a stone, I cannot speak,
I don't know what I'm doing.

Worse than falling into a heavy sea,
worse than the biggest wave of the sea,
to be smashed down again and again,
face broken, head empty, staggering,
propelled into a wall of obsidian.

Hit the mantle, then fixed and dumb,
caught in the mineral density of loss;
katabasis to the core, the shadow zone
then turning, her hand on his shoulder
lighter than – gone, and then turning, gone.

*

If I could assemble the shadows and light
which lie in the folds of your discarded clothes,

the pink jacket with pearlised buttons,
the red jacket for work, the black dress like a wave;

their syntax would speak the life we hold in our hands,
show the shape of you I know and slow the running film.

If I were a lark and could rise to sing
I would write my love a letter we all might understand.

Awe fee us
       sing it
out of dancing darkness
       sing it.

*

From the garden we see the stars turning
and we're sure that these words won't fly;
I was thinking rather of the silver birch
sweet and limby reaching out in the night.

There it shows green again, green sparks,
I was thinking rather of you, your face
staring up steadily in the lit doorway
and the taste of you filling my mouth.

No man looks at me like you, you really look;
and there goes the song running for the exit,
the mystery dance slides us across the floor
flips the order of things in the inhabited world.

I see you with my hands, the colour of your stare
in dark rooms, eyes open, stroke by stroke aswim,
a night spent turning the day inside out,
late late writing the book of wonders.

Footnote to the above

Above the sparkling sea displayed
on the stone steps rising to the chapel
permanent black marker boxed in white
– FILIA KOK SUSTS –

From here the Messenian gulf receives
the meeting of the Aegean and middle sea;
a short way out the water is 4 miles deep,
unnamed bioluminescent forms thrive.

Under darkness village dogs bark in Greek,
dog counterpoint shreds the starry sky;
the waves turn and turn about, barely tidal,
barely tidal the stain on the harbour wall.

*

A black boat makes for the east,
a long slow wake opening a V
on water almost glutinous.

They sit fixed and unfixed in their story,
she stares back at the past of her past;
a man's face, a city of men, blanched.

The sky blazes and the sea boils red,
they breathe darkness into themselves
and can't keep their hands off one another.

That morning on the shallow indentations,
dazed and lolling, they scoop out each other
with no sense of what's solid, what liquid.

They don't talk but stare and scoop;
the coast recedes and bearings reverse,
the boat slides forward into the risen sun.

*

That night in the silent city
the gates closed and fires low
Helen walked around the horse.

She ran her hands on its flanks
stroked the charge and clicked an X-ray
of the crouching men patted into slaughter.

Her mouth brushing the grain of the wood
whispered their names in the voices of their wives
and they saw the shape her lips would make.

Old red horse, battered, flaking,
where are we now?
What whispers inside you?

We've crossed the Trojan plain,
rolled through the gate
let's do what we do.

*

We hang suspended above the city,
jigsaw pieces thrown into the air;
the islands and the sea, the Periclean hills,
the Parthenon and Syntagma Square unconstituted,
flicker and fall in bright array as time stops.

Those relationships of men and women turn over and over,
collapse into Saronic blue, the arms of the darkening coast
under the flood of stars over the Argolid and Arcadia;
falling and falling we fear nothing, only the end of thought,
to be layered in dust, seeing Phidias and the face of Athena.

*

Lydian luxury: the invention of coinage
sent seismic ripples pelagic,
electrum wrinkling the face of the Aegean
made the whole world a subduction zone.

Lydia on the caravan routes of the east,
flooding the Maiandros and Hermos Valleys,
whispered, *man is money* in Smryna,
ships head west on the old conditions dissolved

Unload debt slavery and economic facts,
the propensity for genocide on the borders,
a handsome stranger at the door ready to trade,
commodities rise and fall singing their own song.

Look what I've got, said Croesus, hands blazing,
my treasure house, my flashy power,
my lion and bull imprinted on your palm;
the abstract weight fits, shaping all you hold.

*

Eleanor at the taverna that night saying
– Of course the government has a plan B,
we run this business, even we have a plan B,
you see, they have a plan what to do, if if if.

People are tir/ed, years the money going,
how long now is this, not knowing what?
So now €200 is a lot, it was 500, but is a lot,
a lot more than nothing, people are tir/ed.

(Plan B) Dog poets of the Mani bark your lot,
send up your poem of despair unmeasured,
slung into the dome of night your distress flares
fall to the ground burning and you bark bark.

*

The David Lynch carpet squares the corridor
red and black out of sight to the lifts of crisis design.

The Euro Bank ATM in geometric shadow
flashes without a queue at 2 in the morning.

Stray cars, Periclean hills stripped bare, Solon gone
O City, suburb of Kifisia, the neighbourhood of power.

Think hard about what you angle for.

*

I saw an island on the mainland
trees by the waves, the south breathing
from Lebanon on Tyrian seas.

I saw the king of the wet drive his car
over soundless calm and the city of Cadmus
it looked like starry sex or Memphis.

He entered the women's apartments
sought the unguarded chamber of Europa,
she was long-gone ferried to the west.

Fountains spouted and fell unattended
desire sprinkled over the earth
and Dionysus sang a hymn to himself.

The party over, why was he there at all?
There was a girl and he was lovesick,
the cestus cinched around his sticky heart.

Comeuppance had him saying anything
just to have her in the springy woods,
reproaching the sky and darling cedars.

I will give you Bacchants for your bridechamber
and satyrs for your chamberlains,
I will make my mind a parade dancing in the street.

Girl, you have the blood of Cypris,
I will I will – all the old jibber jabber,
rejected he left with a thought of Ariadne.

He quit Asia for the cities of Europe,
to rattle the palace of Pentheus
and ready another scatter dance.

Common Measure

Letter to Arov Manttir

1

I wanted to write though you're far away;
out here I'm stuck on this upturned bowl
walking the white bones of the peninsula
under a booming dome of blue.

I don't know the year the season the rhythm
but sense there's no linkage across the sky,
no route around the circuit of daily town
where cyclopean walls fell in the last tremour.

So we're laid open to the sea on three sides,
the wavering world crowds back and forth
lapping at the shore piecemeal and frigid,
and I dream myself anchored in capital certainty.

But the assurance of big knowing has run dry,
a-stutter on the narrow exegesis up the slippery hill
abandoned to the bespattering birds and beasts;
we're belated, spitting dust, scornful by default.

On this arid tongue of no tune nothing flows,
we dance up and down the mouth music scales
like a brittle ladder lofted into the night,
foot on the first rung you can't see the top.

Deserted by the advocates of desiccated speech
I'm embarrassed to say how meaning is spilt,
leaking corrosive in the streets for paddling youth
– but forgive me my fault, this is a night rant only.

Saying what you thought cost you everything,
your ingenious mouth sewn shut and buried;
an audience of white rocks arranged in a circle
night curving darker from island to island.

Pitched into silence I track the lighthouse sweep
in the undergrowth fauna glint and retreat;
the sea for which there's no fixed term
bears everything in the burden of its song.

2

I lay awake again last night
into the hours of don't look,
I remembered their cities
where you must wait and be still.

Power seeps from their houses
from their banks and commissions,
across the pretty night square
I saw you stand up a world away.

In the little drifts of autumn
you made ready the speaking forest
like Russian music on the march
against their rancid craft.

You made ready the speaking forest,
and in truth you said - dump the poetry.
Tell me Arov what's the thread here?
What matters in the end?

She stood in the light of the doorway,
she was still and I stepped through the door;
the rest of my life I heard the first song
and walked in the light of that street.

The first song we always hear
is the shape that language takes
around the charged earth referential,
a substance made in all we make.

A small boy sat on the forest floor,
the forest was in a foreign country
he didn't know that, he just sat there
and his heart was full.

In the drift of leaves falling
he looked up through tall trees,
the leaves fell to his hands a wonder
and his heart was full.

3

Thank you for the account of your situation
what you say of the single gate barring the way
suspended and locked to turn the click of exile,
the very ground cast in shadow confirms it all.

How the houses of power blaze long into the night
wrinkle the brown river upon which they sit;
there's a dark trick to authority like that
but here it's made manifest and unashamed.

Your two recent ballads strike home
Barbarians in the Capital and The Border Guard's Lament;
I can't decide which best states the case
against massive, predictable orchestration.

Imagine erosion of the terms of resistance,
the dismemberment of the ethical state;
our betters high on the hog of language drift
making milk and honey from the froth.

The shape of their power is not complex
but a matter of hidden tunnels and loyalties,
the occasional firework display or sticky pageant
bread catapulted over ramparts for plebs.

The second accounts for much of our history,
says who we are is a function of borders;
those others we jig back and forth with hot-foot
to dance the cognates recalling a greater world.

The Ballad is the dream of an objective poetry;
words shaped and weighed released to purpose
the sure steps to the door of the tower,
the door itself neatly fitted and easy to open.

Stepping inside you find the single instrument
set to sound the dream of an objective poetry,
the song of the well-made thing ready to hand
the singer on stage who happened to sing.

4

Arov if I have you right
these messages you send,
with the first snow at the window
and the forgotten song of the sea,
speak the stubborn joy of making.

If I read you right you say

The movement of water shapes
a surfacery lettering, inscribes arcs
and lines to record an intermittent blue,
a path of mineral accumulation
catching the sky over broken land.

If I read you right you say

There's nothing to fear in deep erosion,
the movement of water requires
a specific vocabulary at root;

in the dark heart of the river its metre
speaks of Spring in a different country.

*

Reports of your last whereabouts make no sense,
dead or out of your mind, holed up in a camp,
a reading man, befriended, writing letters for others.
Really, was that you, dropped at the last station,
the slow earth turning an uninhabited sea of grass?

You said – until you're ready to go, stay;
don't look out the door at the frozen tracks,
otherwise you'll never leave;
a scatter of rotting huts, ditches, a fence,
the inventive ways of men with cement.

Time crouching behind a barricade
staring from a wall of forest at the boundary
waiting for the next wave of barbarians;
the single thing that changes are their names.
The rule is ten lines only, the postcards lined.

Everyday you saw the sun decline
into the same trench, everyday you looked
to see there was nothing down there,
everyday the running music effaced.
The rule is ten lines only, the postcards lined.

5

Today the wind falls on the sea like a drunk
and the impossible blue of sky and water meet;
in the shelter of the garden every leaf, every stone
restores sight by doing nothing, and the white path
laid over granite and the bones of the dead is just so.

To see it merely as the edge of the land is a mistake,
forever unrecorded in the end, the descent
over stones, rock pools, beds of seaweed, takes no adept,
without even a dog-faced sceptic of a seal to see you fall
down into a signal-free zone where raging tides contend.

But here Arov I've translated your last message.

Perhaps it's poetry's lot to sing outside the walls
for all it's worth, for company – as if we make a thing
above ourselves in the air apparent as a flight path;
come you cormorants, you tearing gulls, feed and leave,
we're laid open to the sea on every side.

You articulates of air, feed and leave
over the dark device on the horizon
carrying, timber, scrap, a final cargo? I don't know.
And those hired hands graft one country to another,
caught in what contract and conditions of the imagination?

Then nothing but a memory of the bonny gorse,
– and walking beneath the dome of scattered lights
then at last nothing but a memory of the gorse
– and I've no idea of the way, which turn to take
dancing both sides of the road into night.

Leipzig

Listen to Steve Reich's Music for 18 Musicians
for the long, slow descent into Leipzig Halle
through the canopy of pan-European clouds
rucked and pinked across the plains of Saxony.

The first lights of town propose an exact location
of fields bound by roads, the Porsche Werke
and the lake pictures a darkening summer night;
double check dial light pilot, double up you players.

We see from the Stasi headquarters in the Runde Ecke
how Honecker made the state a poem in paranoia;
we see the people of Leipzig who took the streets
standing together, night after night to break an empire;
there the music of Bach rises up into the sky
an architecture of light transparent and exact.

*

Joseph Str 7, Leipzig

Lotrowsky the Jewish baker
of Joseph Strasse, his good bread
popular with his neighbours;
ran a fine bakery.

In Lindenau dreaming Zion
with banners unfurled, dreaming
refugees welcome in this country,
where ghosts trip on stumbling blocks.

An inscribed tile in the pavement
records that life and its ending;
a ruined house allowed to speak
and this was Isaac's garden.

His children played in the street
his wife's name was Ida,
They marched us to the station
with nothing in our hands.

Ida deported to Riga 1942
Anna left for Chile aged 19
Adolf to Brazil 1940
Joseph to Sachsenhausen.

      *

Even if I could hear nothing
and see in a spotlight nothing
but Tamamo Saito's bowing arm
surrounded by unending darkness
and the fingers of her left hand
flicker over the strings of running genius
nor hear a single note of Bach's Partita:
I would know beauty is made.

And then there's light and there's sound
rising on the air of the Nikolai Kirche
and Tamamo Saito's black hair a river
falling over her right shoulder dances
flowing through the intricate ciaconna;
a girl's hands remaking the whole world.

At the Hospital Doors

The sun shines on the Oncology Centre,
the red cars, the grey, the marked-out spaces;
workmen to the site office, patients to reception,
paces vary with purpose at the sliding doors.

Wind from the distant world sifts the borders
and the light lifts but there's no revelation here,
the working night turns into the working day,
deliveries arrive, innocent cells race deranged.

Pain seeps down into faults below ground,
grips the roots of trees with blackened fingers
sounds every note of diving bird song
and directs the shifting clouds not to speak.

Guided by certain hands and quiet talk,
around whose neck are these pearls arrayed?
Little aria little aria in the streets of dark town,
out in the hollows the air of Autumn sings.

*

Three ghosts sing for life
from the white sheets of final care.

I was born in 1920 – I married when?
and then the war, three sons I had, my boys,
my brother died when I was ten,
it grieves me still, that something unfinished.

Well that was me working on the farm,
me and my dad, up the hills, the best school;
though she left me, I love her even still
but oh my daughter's the pillar of my life.

The year? I don't remember. I'll ask Alan,
ah – no, I can't can I, he's gone now
but we had fun, hungry most of the war,
the Mediterranean, salt water out of the taps.

Two women and a man sing for life
moment by moment from their beating hearts,
the miracle of ordinary events recalled
– oh but I miss him, all gone I know.

                    *

We lie in common secluded, curtained for surgery,
paused on the threshold for time to be removed.

I hear a man close-by weighing his life thus far,
hear his words hit the cold pan of the scales.

Let the sincerity in his heart, lighter than a feather
open the doors from the light and from the dark.

Dream Journey

I fell asleep on the train speeding through a long tunnel,
under that mountain those invasive voices came in close
dedicated to their own preferment at every station.

I dreamt there was a Tory government and didn't know the place,
heard dictation from the mirage book of history in self-effacing chorus,
for instance: the nations we helped make are unmaking themselves.

They live in high towers above the river, sparky sparky they circulate
corporate ghost men and women spin spin in their golden circles,
from the centrifuge they measure the bounce in system collapse.

In the archaeology of long occupation the dust of fallen capitals
rises over our heads and shows how even Jerusalem fell upon itself,
Jerusalem the Golden made dumb with a mouthful of ash.

*

Zaventem is open this morning and the flights
come and go again above the suburbs of Brussels,
leaving empty places at the tables of the innocent.

The girl whose feet were severed by the blast,
the boy who saved his mother,
– *No no, stay here, there's always a second bomb.*

She is learning to walk without feet,
he is learning to carry what he saw;
when count is taken of those families nothing will suffice.

Beaming from a box of light Brueghel depicts the living
and Icarus kicks the sea; parachutes, parachutes said St. Michael,
though the landscape of ekphrasis makes no answer.

Ah, the traffic is heavy today, but no said the taxi driver,
I think there is a problem; gridlock, sirens, helicopters,
we sit in stationary cars, everyone looks at everyone else.

*

All morning I've waited on the terrace of this expensive hotel
reading about Mandelstam and the terror, the genius of Nadezhda;
I sit in the European sun as the Spring rain pools on the tables
to stare straight back at the rolling sky, in the air surrounded
by the genius of Nadezhda and the earth our boundless house.

I sit and work and see the planes come in one after another
arriving on an invisible cord, wheels down, ready for business;
the sun flickering their heraldry makes a dancing yellow,
guided in, their song descends from an expanse of blue,
a deepening tone to touchdown in another country.

Common Measure

I walked out one March morning
the wind chasing the sky about;
saw no future, spoke no claptrap
green Spring came up from below.

I kept the polished artefact of it
in a glass of water at the window
the red oxide ran like a river
in the temporary light of day.

Composed of Indo-European words
it would sink roots into the Earth,
the facets – field, king, village, house
washed all a-glitter I saw.

*

A Man Sings from the Bar and Beyond

Another night listening to Iranian Radio Traditional,
Sonati Reliability: Excellent Bit Rate: 12kbps
prompts the song to rise from an unknown world,
a sustained solo on the sandouri closes the distance.

What shape does the language substance take
surrounding the earth to make the shape of what we make?
Those particles of words as if thinking and speaking,
sonati – the fresh water river rolling around all our days.

It casts the news without meaningful captions,
sends children across the world alone, we know this happens;
I hear Peter Riley read from a CD, from a real town
a possible speech carrying its load lightly on the air.

Under a mortal sky medical conditions prevail,
my regular irregular heart beat patters on;

it's not significant Peter, I hear you in all that poetry,
the grand conversation - and snow is promised tomorrow.

*

Dear Sandeep

Sparta Egypt Troy triangulated
What does it take? Helen thought.
She understood something when the boat
hit the iceberg, the grinding nature of
the sound of desire shook everything.

Like the rumour of a golden girl in Sparta
flooded the villages and made men mad.
Seismic Poseidon – You jealous fuck,
let my thoughts dance, what does it take
for my body to follow? Helen sang.

Dear Sandeep, to your unanswered question,
Today Helen would be? Jack the sailor said,
'To make her into an artefact is to try to kill her.'
I don't know, I think she was already there,
we're predisposed and those men already mad.

It seems a harsh sentence and we're charged:
Helen a substance soft on my fingers
and before me above ground walking,
Melanie's vigil over me all night
talking me back to life, *talk, you must talk to me.*

Driven from hell through the body of air
Greek summer full-blown filled the car,
I saw a woman's eyes and moving mouth,
a way of going about the world, of deciding
what Helen would know and the shape she would take.

*

Melanie you gave me back my life when we met
and saved my life when I fell to the embolism spooks.

I think of you, the dark conspiracy of your body,
when you're gone I'm a stripped pale man who sleeps alone.

I hunger for you, that you are there, proportionate, complete;
if I could explain this it would be an irresistible music.

Sing those slow songs to me as night comes on
from your beautiful face, from your moving mouth.

As you in your life make decisions in the world
sing me those slow songs from your mouth.

                    *

Let's walk out in common measure
the fit of your hand in mine
the ground falls away at every step
the circuit of Spring unfolding.

Let's walk to the next turn,
you know that place we came to
where woven sound of sea and air
ballads the chambered ground.

A Greek Spring

The Costa NeoRomantica sits in Kalamata harbour
a brightly lit toppling wedding cake of eight decks
above the darkened immiserated town of the Peloponnese.

Sister to the Costa Concordia it carries the grey heads of Europe
to cruise the Mediterranean promising luxury and classical ruins,
that this ship floats at all seems improbable.

The passengers see the outline of the Taygetos on a clear night
and will sail to the Piraeus and the ancient capitals of the East,
they're not here to see where an economy has landed in cataclysm.

On the Costa NeoRomantica a crew of 622 serve 1,600 guests,
the public rooms are furnished in rare woods and Carrara marble
and the walls drip with original works of art worth millions of dollars.

Alcaeus, Sophocles, Aeschylus and Plato launched the metaphor
but may not have envisaged the ship of state cruising thus
and I don't reclaim it for the fleet of the Carnival Company plc.

*

Spring of fornicating pigeons hot-foot on the wires
back and forth to the tower of Captain Christeas,
they measure and clip the coming riot.

Spring of painting stones to protect the Oleander,
Yourgos paints his boat to make ready for summer
everything seen in the green haze rising from the earth.

At night lights low on the water set out in darkness,
three lights, a one-man fishing boat, a living;
and elsewhere on the other side of the same small sea

Pity those who take the 25 minute crossing,
pity those who make it and those who don't,
25 minutes, $1,500 sailing into darkness.

Spring of everything rising from the earth
Spring of everything drowning in sight of land
the air a chamber of birdsong wide as the sky.

*

Outside the plate glass windows of Country Burger on E65
the Spring sun lifts over the plains and valleys of the Argolid,
light flooding the green panorama of deep memory.

Agamemnon lies under that hill, Orestes runs the hidden pass
and the radio sings – you will find me, time after time
but there's no western music for this moment.

The Spring green inundation of the golden Argolid.

Lee Harwood 1939-2015

1

Lee in the high room, Ward 9A East
with a view of the Brighton Sea,
the sound of July's children playing
as a coastal breeze taps at the window.

I drove long tunnels of swaying trees
through Gloucestershire and Oxfordshire,
and walked the hospital maze to find him
through green underwater light made blind.

There quietly asleep, my friend and poet
who gave us space in which to breathe,
that poetry could be like this too;
I touched his arm – *Oh Kelvin you made it.*

Short of breath and *ah the names escape me
no matter,* he knew what was happening,
a handful of poets to keep and his children
he held them there like the pull of gravity.

*

Lee on the mountain, above Llŷn Ogwen say,
the mist parting, Paul's there and it's alright;
no rescue required, no Rope Boy at the ready,
just the clear view and the mountain at his feet.

Reading he casts his artful net,
where have we come, where is this?
I thought it was simple but here…
time has been folded and then let run.

Passing on the late train he waves,
sporting his official British Rail scarf;

the blue and red script of a better country
streams out like a banner across the Downs.

The light from the guards van recedes,
the train slips into a pocket of memory;
he's seeing the last passenger home,
making ready for the next shift.

2

The bees are heavy in the Polygala
and the sure-footed lizard climbs the wall,
the heat rolls slow waves off the sea
and abandons itself to layered silence
– he would have liked its colour, a Harwood blue.

The slightest breeze slips into the house
and my mind's made white for staring,
what I thought I wanted to say drifts and sinks,
the postcard sent too late, an old, blue, Greek lorry;
– Look it's me driving, where do you want to go?

To think of talking to him is like this now,
an unaddressed postcard sent into the world;
the stamp looked like toppling slices of melon,
he would have liked it, considered its provenance;
the people of Melonitsa singing late into the night.

The Melonitsans are poor and own next to nothing
but on festive days gather around the central square;
each citizen brings one precious thing to hold aloft,
then improvises a song, though the rules are strict;
if favoured all others sing a rousing chorus and cheer.

Lee, the bees are heavy in the Polygala
and the sure-footed lizard climbs the wall.

3

At breakfast in the high room at home
light playing across the ceiling,
in the street people walk by and talk.

The sea's just down the road to the right,
the white band of the sea and all the world
making its song for him to follow.

Have you heard this cd? Rafe sent it, it's marvellous
and here's that book I was talking about
and this is how I will think of you alive.

*

He stands under the dark tower now,
the sea drags its only word back and forth,
a dog barks half the night, a train approaches;
he waits, turns to listen, courteous to the living.

4

Drinking to the mighty dead in the arms of the queen,
the day rises sea-washed and fit for riding to the end,
with Botallack fallen into sea surge and the sky in ribbons
we're on the tilt, the frame the course was set by broken.

Hereabouts generations of men slipped underground,
the Bal Maidens above unsheltered, spalling the ore;
livings made and lives lost for mineral truth, for tin,
hereabouts the song runs into the earth, the hidden adit.

From below you hear the sea breaking on the shore,
a continuous muffled speech without meaning;
to picture the world from this sound is unthinkable,
the dust-filled air, the empty cup, only restate thirst.

Lee I object to your death – I object to death? How useless
to fight the dark apprenticeship with hands tied;
but drink to the mighty dead on a bright day in Botallack,
where the Atlantic rolls a chorus and gathers unbearable light.

*

Yesterday we walked from Zennor to Pendeen Watch,
tramped the white stones of the path and turfy moor;
two girls swam in the cove, a hovering kite for company,
for colour late foxgloves, seathrift and sea-wash changes.

We dropped into a pocket of silence below the clifftop,
then, step by step, the sound of the sea returned on the air
as we rose out of the hollow and distance laid its claim;
this would have done, it was just right for Lee to join us.

But his delight remains untaken, he'll not stand to see
the sunlit hill towards Morvah, Tor Noon and the Carn,
the exact detail of the Celtic fields green and yellow,
the blue curve of the moor, the band of light to the west.

So I can only imagine him at the kitchen window
up early, asking – *What do you think that bird is there?*

*

and always the sea and the
hills sloping down to the sea

The sea drew that man into itself
into the formless body of water
through a brimming submarine zero.

We're all bound for Boston
so haul away boys, haul away
though I doubt we'll find him there.

Farewell the good man Harwood
farewell our fairest friend
come morning we'll see no land in sight.

Radio Archilochos

Ραδιόφωνο Αρχίλοχος

'Of the Greek poets of the seventh century BC
we know almost nothing and none of their
poems has come down to us entire.'
Guy Davenport

1

What am I doing here far from Paros,
as if I've fallen from radiant thought?
The whole place is out of season, buried,
the crested grey wave curls under a grey sky.

Thasos is always out of season, stuff it;
all the signs say how far it is to elsewhere
in a thickening Thracian jibber-jabber;
it's harder to find the unreachable here.

I would be a sober border guard, walk the line.
What border? A nest of rats squeaking – *mamma.*
No seriously, tell me what we are doing here?
A better source of nutritious nuts and pig meat?

I watch the waterfront; see the trade come and go,
sit with the washed-up and fashionably wasted;
they assume a witty commentary, make much of little,
their daughters and goods shipped out the back door.

*

Another cold night, the moon high, a small coin
tossed for a cheap scene over hills and sea;
an old woman shouts at the dogs by her door,
they bark and circle and she stops shouting,
and they bark: it's hardly the matter of elegy.

Yesterday a new boat arrived – Golden Dawn,
Shit Day followed by Fucked-Up Night, more like.
When we're gone, what will these Thasians do?
Fall on each other? Forget how to cultivate grapes?
Let the mines collapse and trouble the goats?

Isolated camps, a few hovels, smoke pours out;
spin my shield to your mates, I'll buy another;

that gap in the wall's not topped by my face.
It was a sweet night, the frogs set up their choir
and the sea all around us rolling in silver.

*

None of this is so,
just figures of air
for a theatre forgotten,
dust replaces ritual.

I did none of these things,
not even the sea rinses the mind
nor dancing on its sliding steps;
we're spume, froth, trappings.

In the dark heart of night
only regret is real.
I watch you sleep, the light
pools around your face.

*

These mainlanders, their Thracian cunning,
will adapt quite readily, smile and serve,
acquire new rhetoric, kill us when they can;
there's nothing broken in them
unlike the chippy trash at the harbour.

So much for strollers and playboys,
the clueless pimps of the academy.
In what sanctuary will his name sound,
before they debauch it with assignations
and let their dogs foul the floor?

We suffered the great provocation
of the greening of the season,
saw pictographs arranged by the leaves:

Gloukos is dead – what do I need now?
Grey slab; I write his name a final time.

*

On the morning air a film rises
by which all is made clear
a ghost I drift anacoluthon
tread the marble bones of Thasos.

Intricate white fingers articulate
a dense forest, shafts of light
fall deep in the pines to the sea floor
where the wavering world says naught.

At this turn of the path something
though there's no-one here,
the frayed air sifting shadows
and I walked the river of stones.

*

I saw today the river of stones
white and cursive under the sun, terraces
and the separate compartments of the gods,
such is our morning calendar.

We make ready, loiter, polish our kit,
look at us scrawny cats of the village;
mostly we wait, sleep and remember
licking our lips at mechanical birds.

When I was a boy running about the house,
he, my father, dreamt a thalassokratia,
looked at the sliding sea's crests and dark gaps
and came up with this, his master plan.

A Thasos of the mind, fat and ripe at the crossroads,
the Black Sea trade, Lydia, the young Greek states,
the gold mines of Mount Pangaeum, timber for ships;
and once I was a boy running about the house.

*

So I sit and drink the Thracian wine
before they export the life out of it;
a slow sunset stretches over half the sky,
in what broken mode behind those clouds?
I don't know, I skipped music lessons.

It looks like her arms and legs opening pink,
d d d delight I taste doesn't begin to say it.
Do you think I could have had a life at home,
unobserved content, she with beauty in her bones?
When I'm gone I would hover over such scenes.

The children of the harbour are like dust swirling,
sparrows skittering, happy and dirty as you like;
they scratch their names in our fortifications,
run and fetch until dark, then those with homes leave;
what the others do until morning I've no idea.

Here's a secret, we're smashed on Ismaric mesmeric
and in the bottom of every cup I find a poem waiting;
Exarchos I lead the dithyramb and climb the walls,
my friend in his old slippery dance calls from Paros,
he doesn't give a fig for me on the killing field.

So we fuck and fight rolling across the taverna floor,
though it might be the ceiling, the world's upside down,
a fine place to meet Lady Muse, dabbing her lips so cool;
the boys collapse in a circle, grinning and unmanned,
come on, I'll sing the lead, I know the words out of here.

*

Boys it's not the easiest number
to be favoured of the muses,
a lyre for the cow didn't please the old man,
he spelt it out in stripes across my arse
for all Apollo and the dancing ones might say.

So come, let's sing another song of home,
we dregs of the Aegean drained to Thasos,
a confluence of half-wits and brutes
it swills about our thighs in triple shit town;
the young wag up to his eyes, marked for death.

*

Do you make of me
the landless bastard son
fit only for the fighting
shelled versions of versions?

The aristocrat dilettante
with a taste for rough trade
and my smart name means
top dog of the squad?

I am The Man I am I claim
to please the boys in the clinch;
think all the dirty work we did
tropes cast in blank memory?

The sun shines, the day rises,
spear points are sharper still,
gold bearing streams run to the sea;
how many voices, four, five, six?

*

Our settlement extended from the harbour
the new markets and fortified base;

we built sanctuaries to Dionysus and Poseidon,
an open-air precinct in the name of Artemis
for commerce of gods and keen men.

There was even, for some to step back in time,
a rock-cut relief of Pan piping to his goats,
floral honey from the high grasslands,
woodlarks, nightjars, birdsfoot trefoil,
pine, yew, prickly juniper and ash.

But Melkarth, seafarer, where were you?
Will we lose this taste for the wealth of others,
this voluptuous itch to have the unknown?
For answer: empire over empire to the horizon,
I saw a mountain turned upside down for gold.

*

Listen you priests and pretty virgins
arrayed in precious stones and gold,
our trade from the east is skinny girls,
stretched-out boys for business men to bore.

You need to know this so drop the shock,
this is the competition you'll face at home;
and there are family estates to settle
and the children of empire to make ready.

As for the thalassokratia blueprint
it was commanded from Delphi
found a new city far-seen, such advice costs;
but Delphi is a sound investment bank.

2

[papyrus   top right corner torn
three words remain
                    wrappings Alexandria]

sparks in wheat
[   ] take
[   ] heart and what
you have
               too tattered to read

Thasos
calamitous city

*

even old men
        wanted them
Gloukos my boy
their cunts
                    again papyrus torn
perfume [   ] for most part
conjecture
               from the shuttered house

*

Athena . . make me strong
come down   [un]surrounded   (embraced in battle?)
a sea of spears catch at
the sky … ? day (light)   (in holes, shreds?)
fields of corpses stink

*

. . my kingfisher
morning darling
she flatters my stump . .

*

from the shattered house [illegible] out
smoke   gone . . those kids
(in the mouths?) of Thracian dogs

*

. . little muse little muse
dancing on the table
on donkey humpback island

I see your eyes sliding
but will you come away
to Paros of the radiance?

*

the dead flat . . (lie in?)
                pools of shit
(and) don't choke [   ] skim slime   [left side torn vertically]
remember us   killing field
javelins out   earth
remember (us)

*

I in darkness thinking light
she [torn] of shadow (form of?)   (body of shadows?)
stepped out …
                unarmed – night
                melting (her)
soft fig (pliant?)
                perfumed

*

call the shop for a new shield
I chucked mine in the hot scrap
ran for dear life on good legs
a treasure (ακριβῶς ακριβός)

*

. . came to the dark shore
the one light/star/fire – she
burning   the one thing I know . .

3

When we first came to the village we were befriended by three children; Clea, Romana and Fiorella. The families, Albanian perhaps, rented a house at the back of the harbour. The girls would pester to play on our bikes and we gave in. They would circle the square, stretching for the pedals and then make off for hours. They broke the gears and punctured the tyres repeatedly. How? I don't know, I've no idea where they found an assault course of nails to ride over. Their mothers would say – thank you for letting them use the bikes, hand on heart, a slow nod. Our pleasure.

On New Year's Eve the girls lined up at our gate and sang to bless the house – for sweets. St. Basil with your alphabet of sticks, bless the house and a long life to all living there, the lady and the man. It's an old custom quickly learnt. As they grew older the village shrank around them and they're gone elsewhere. Clea, the brightest I think, was learning English, the ticket out. Clea, Romana and Fiorella young women now, somewhere in that other world. Cross the New Year's Cake with a knife. Cut the first piece for Christ and then for the poor, next the host, his wife and the family, beginning with the oldest.

*

That summer the reinvention of poverty was very apparent. The English woman running car hire in the next village agreed, there were fewer labourers around, fewer builders. For several decades Albanians have been the casual labour and skilled house builders in parts of rural Greece. She thought that most had left; Albania was a better prospect now. She shrugged and said – *Well, Greeks have always had slaves haven't they, they'll find some more.* This is an uncluttered, plain view of history. We were having this conversation in Messenia, the slave grounds for Sparta. An older, harder pattern has returned. The young are leaving. The surface style of mainstream European expectations is being effaced. Driving across the Peloponnese on the big, post-Olympic empty roads the towns looked like a war had rolled by and just stopped from exhaustion.

Late one night we heard rembetika, the Levantine blues, sneaking out of a narrow street. For drinks, two young men and an older man were performing outside a kafaneio. The old man was missing several fingers, a typical injury for fishermen who dynamite the fish to make catching them easier. The music had its sardonic growl, its bite, its pissed-offness and weary companionship. The young men and the old man all knew the same songs. We'd slipped back decades to earlier bad times; the population exchange in 1923, the war, the civil war. That the crisis is good for rembetika is no comfort to the newly poor. The bloody minded singing, its mode of bitterness tells you about this dark continuity.

*

I saw a poster today, taped to a post. It was a picture of a politician, fair but with dark eyes and a dreamy look. He appeared almost feminine or perhaps a forgotten descendant of Atatürk. He had that smile; if snakes could smile it would be learnt from him. There were slogans in red print sending the blame elsewhere; anything will do to short circuit thought. Apparently to make things better, right to the top, we must pursue the policies which led us here. Those already at the top must stay put, for their expertise in getting us here. This is called the new way, a revolution in the halls of the capital. These posters come ready faded, soon tattered and the print bleeds.

*

Continuity runs deeply. We went late one night to a performance in the amphitheatre at Epidaurus. The play was Heracles by Euripides, and the acoustics are astonishing. From the centre spot of the circular orchestra you can hear the merest whisper to the top of the 54 tiers of seating and, perhaps, spreading out over the Argolid hills; the original psychorama to the plays themselves. The theatre has been there since the 4th century BC. The original capacity was 15,000. I think there were approximately 10,000 of us there that night.

The sky darkened, the play began and we became near silent. Heracles returns from his labours, releases his wife and children from captivity by the usurper Lycus. All's well. And then Heracles is made mad and slaughters his family – and by now it is very dark. Several moments in the play brought us back to present conditions. One in particular was well received. Amphitryon, father of Heracles, updates him on the situation in Thebes.

There's a large class of needy men, who make a show
Of being prosperous; Lycus has their strong support.
They raised the riots; they sold Thebes to slavery
In hope of lawless plunder, to redeem their own
Bankruptcy, caused by extravagance and idleness.

But the play is two and a half thousand years old, removed from us by translation and cultural specifics, and besides everything is different now.

*

A history of empire is reflected in the vulgarly attuned face of the patrician poster boy. You can't look into the drilled gaze of his eyes because there's nothing there; the thinking has already gone to the future. His introspection is about imitating and replacing the life deliberately destroyed and on the back of which he rises. A version of the good times, always in the past and always coming soon, is bundled on a handcart to market for people to buy, to reacquire what was taken from them in the first place. The old perish and the young leave to sing sad songs on scut wages in the very countries whose bankers burnt their homes and stole their economy.

*

After a night and day of storms, of a hot off-shore wind at force 9 flattening the sea to hammered tin, scalping the pepper tree and littering most of the garden across the courtyard floor; the old women come out of their doors to talk. About what? Their business, the price of dog food, what goes on in Athens? Where's Yannis got to with the fish van? He's no good, like his uncle, the one who had the donkey. The dogs play fight under the tower and the woman across the square joins in the talk, laying it down. Andonis fiddles with his moped to get it going. The sea's roar is a murmur and the renewed sun picks out every leaf, every surface, every hovering insect.

4

Crossing a big sea   (24)
in a toy boat
κατεστάθην.
I am restored
to the light of day.

ἀμφικαπνίουσιν
They will surround with smoke   (89)
blinded
hacked at
drained to
feed the earth.

[θεσσάμενοι] γλυκερὸν νόστον
A sweet homecoming   (8)
Paros open your arms
make soft your marble bed
night by night illuminated
spoon me your pleasures.

ἀκόντων δοῦπον
Thud of javelins   (139)
exhaled bone
of white atoms
a small cloud
forms no word
where you stood
sucked backwards
into black zero.

[Ὡς] κηρύλος
A kingfisher   (41)
flicks its wings
delight flutters
wrapped in her
nectar flows.

γῆ φόνωι χλκ ονδενηεδ[
The earth with blood   (91)
the fields of the dead
spread but nothing grows
bones   slippery guts
on which you build a town

Παρδακὸν δ᾽ ἐπείσιον
Wet cunt   (40)
from the lord of moistness
I walk I swim drenched
the field entangled   she is
always blessed wet Dionysus.

τί μοι μέλει ἀσπὶς ἐκείνη;
Abandoned shield   (5)
added mine
to the big display
growing on
a pretty bush

γυναικῶν
Of women   (10)
of the water
of women
I drank.

73

Ἐμοὶ τόθ' ἥδε γῆ χ[άνοι].
May the earth [   ] for me   (220)
gape wide
χ[άνοι].)
earth
hold my tongue
let go the sting
earth
my last vessel.

5

South then the circle island's candid calling,
a boat-load of tumescent men going home
awash with it, steaming and propelled;
the girls of home flexible, keen from absence;
come on boys, Paros is worth a rash.

South then for the circle island's soft calling;
let's make two colours of the whole business,
the blue, the white, the joy of entering port;
the water churning transparent as thought
we shoot the fast channel for home.

*

I devised the elegiac couplet, iambic and trochaic meters,
dimeter to tetrameter, epodes and asinarteta;
I wrote I every day and coined the term reggae.

And yes I liked a good fight, Ares at my side;
it's true I had the hot sister, the lively younger one,
bragged on every chat show; swing Lycambes swing.

It's also true that critical reception has been mixed;
I was considered quarrelsome and foul-mouthed,
a lascivious, common bastard – or something like that.

It's a bright Spring morning, the air is scented and moist,
all around the little birds are fornicating;
the Naxian who will kill me is eating his breakfast.

*

That sense of something there in the charged air,
I think Apollo Hylates is curving the words to himself,
I think he's got the green eye on my stranger, my darling;
though he'll protect my name against the bad mouths.

The young get Dionysus of course, and don't need him,
possessed of riot, burning day and earth's pulse;
they don't need dancing gods or a presence in the trees,
their moment is unbearable, endlessly pursued, complete.

I built a temple here to the slippery one, sang him up,
sang him up from the streets dressed in iamb and elegy;
the sea like a thought lapping at the marble shore,
our days of figs and seafaring, of honey in the pot.

But unlike H I never had the big sweep,
that epic arrogance to make much of little
– ten years for one woman, come off it;
I rise and fall with sporadic song abounding.

Good spear strike home, cut to epode restored or no;
the tip is worked bronze, balanced, good for slashing,
one, two, fast as you like, opened face, point's made;
though I'd rather be an old dog dreaming in the sun.

Above all else I swear bad poetry will do for me,
the lickspittle decrepitude of our lolling tongue;
after invasion and the markets going yoyo mental
etymology alone counts, crooks make snot of words.

I keep faith in ellipses without reaching for proof
but I'm lost and nowhere between the songs,
a blindness of another kind, a different periplus,
an archipelago of girls in a milky sea.

*

In Candid Town where I was born
there was a young maid dwelling,
stroked for epode she caught my breath.

76

We knew her name, her father and all that,
not to see her was like death in the street
not to be looked at by her even worse.

In the hot maze of alleyways and markets
the light buds around her and feeds the earth,
step into this darkness darling, let's play gods.

We can cast the nets of pleasure all night,
a gentle pull, a touch here to ease the living thing,
it comes with many names and I know a few.

I only follow your lead, over the wall, into the meadow,
you choose I stumble after, unstrung but for your word;
from my thought you've already wiped all other women.

Even if the goddess were your sister I would be blind.
Shall we shoot the milky stars in the Parian night?
Come let me lay down my special cloak for you.

I have a memory of a girl in a field when I was a boy,
there's nothing like a girl in a spring meadow
tremulous as the April wind rippling her garden.

Your tender breasts, belly and dark cunt
shaping my tongue to our first language;
your eyes and mouth hesitant shed glory on the earth.

I would unravel from you, from your dewy skin
what will be wrapped around a rotted corpse;
papyrus girl, be unafraid, be untranslated.

All the flowers, their little faces dancing to the goddess,
and me, the fool in flood, losing it on the temple steps;
well, let me leave it as a tribute sweetheart.

Pressed against your shape, your colour it gives again;
you were always what I wanted and I'll come back for more,
that you are in the world answers the big question for me.

That you are in my arms slowly turning is even better,
head down on my steady hand, look at me you said
then you glanced over your shoulder and whispered – I need this.

*

From here the ways of Paros
and the sea where the sun goes
to the bounds of the inhabited world,
I keep my feet in the hearth.

What is out there I know,
sweet waters of Siris flow
those islands of furthest blue
waiting for their names.

What is out there I know;
Leophilos friend of the people
Leophilos shiny face all over the shop;
let me translate the future tense.

But I've no spear in my hand,
no swooping crow in my heart;
I'm done with all that, it appears
I reveal this to you here.

*

It's surely a joke that after Thasos, after everything,
I died on Paros at the hands of a Naxian?

Calondas you crow – what do crows eat for breakfast?
Do you see this letter postmarked Hades?

Well I have precedent there with Demeter;
so listen, this is what will happen to you:
my gods can strike the censorious limp,
make the bridegroom impotent and pale.

But you at Delphi will get the elbow from the god,
how does that taste as you flit down Parnassus?
It tastes like shit doesn't it – you fuck:
crows eat their own guts, eating kills them.

*

She held a flag of myrtle and the rose
and stepped softly from the shadows.

Do you know me? I said, and stared,
I'm the first person to write in the first person.

Really? Well the price is still the same,
for you and your friend, Exarchos or not.

*

Last night there was dancing,
thunder rattled down to the sea
and the local trio struck up.

One ancient granddad played the goat
step stop stop – pause, stop motion, shot
and sprang back into it like a boy.

The sinuous girls bending, steady eyed,
untouchable, make the air a substance,
faces lit up and glistening.

Dionysus from our village dances,
and the music circulates intoxicated,
an enclave of light on the mountain.

*

Archilochos, his voice broken, sits collapsed,
legs splayed on the soft bed of summer dust;
a spear sticks out of his chest, its black length
rises and dips with his last breath and the next.

His last sight those grey stumpy olive trees
or figures of final truth paused by the track,
and below him lies all the geology of Paros
where young marble giants wait to take their form.

Get up, get up Archilochos we need your bite;
will you bring us the news, say who benefits this time?
Archilochos has gone to the rushing night, the dark sea,
he hovers one moment in the light over Antiparos.

Notes

The Abduction Zone

Helen whispering to the Greeks inside the Trojan horse see *The Odyssey*, IV, 277–289.

Common Measure

In Leipzig The Stumbling Block project memorialises victims of the Holocaust. Their names are written on small brass tiles embedded in the pavement near their former homes.

In the second part of the poem 'Common Measure' I'm talking to two poems by Peter Riley, 'The Little Watercolour at Sligo' and 'That Grand Conversation Was Under the Rose' from *Passing Measures*, 2000. In the third part I'm addressing Sandeep Parmar and her book *Eidolon*, 2015. 'To make her into an artifact is to try to kill her.' is from Jack Spicer's poem 'Helen: A Revision.'

The quotation in the final part of 'Lee Harwood 1939-2015' is from *Boston-Brighton*, Lee Harwood, 1977.

Radio Archilochos

For the ten archaic Greek terms from Archilochos in part 4, and for his generous and expert guidance, many thanks to Paschalis Nikolaou of the Ionian University. The numbers in this part of the poem refer to the fragments of Archilochos in *Greek Iambic Poetry*, edited and translated by Douglas E. Gerber, Loeb Classical Library, 1999.

What we know about Archilochos is found in the fragments of his poetry which remain. He came from Paros and lived from c.680 – c.640 BC, possibly. His father, Telesicles, led the Parian colonisation of Thasos. *Possibly* hovers over every assertion about Archilochos. He was either the son of this influential family or an illegitimate mercenary; either way he saw military service on Thasos. He is credited with several poetic innovations and is renowned for his use of what could be autobiographical experience; or possibly not, as such details could just as well be the formal moves in a set of aesthetic conventions unknown to us. He may well have played a key role in the cult of Dionysus on Paros. Archilochos was killed by a Naxian whose name meant crow; the circumstances of this act are unknown.